On the Contrary

On the Contrary

Poems by
Lia Sturua

———————•———————

translated by
Natalia Bukia-Peters
and Victoria Field

fal

Poems © Lia Sturua
Translations © Natalia Bukia-Peters and Victoria Field
Introduction © Natalia Bukia-Peters and Victoria Field

ISBN 978-0-9555661-8-9

First published in 2023 by

fal publications
9 The Crescent
Canterbury
CT2 7AQ
UK

www.falpublications.co.uk

Printed by TJ Books Ltd, Padstow

Design and layout Bob Carling

Cover photograph Dina Oganova

Acknowledgements

The translators would like to thank Lia Sturua and the Writers' House of Georgia for making this book a reality, and, especially, Irine Chogoshvili for her support, friendship and patience over our many years of working together.

Five of these poems, some in slightly different versions, previously appeared in *A House with No Doors: Ten Georgian Women Poets* translated by Natalia-Bukia-Peters and Victoria Field (Francis Boutle, 2016).

This book is published with the support of the Writers' House of Georgia.

Writers' House of Georgia
Iv. Machabeli str. 13, 0105, Tbilisi, Georgia

Writers' House of Georgia

Contents

Introduction

This book presents a selection of poems from Lia Sturua's two most recent published collections and some which have been published in magazines. The selection of poems for this book was made by Lia herself.

We were struck by the timelessness of Lia Sturua's poetry. Georgian critic, Maia Jaliashvili, wrote, 'In real time and space, Lia Sturua belongs to the twentieth and twenty-first centuries, but metaphorically speaking, in imaginary, virtual dimensions, she is part of eternity'. Her poems seem to belong to what in ancient Greek is termed *kairos*, the eternal, or opportune moment.

Of course, poets themselves live in chronological time. Lia Sturua was born in 1939. This was the year when, as the Spanish Civil War came to an end, Hitler invaded Poland. It was when war broke out between Hungary and Slovakia, and Italy invaded Albania. Stalin, an ethnic Georgian, born in Gori in 1878, was pursuing his policies of Russian nationalism across the Soviet Union to curb dissent. The people of Ukraine had recently experienced mass starvation and genocidal deportations. In Georgia, members of the Blue Horns, a group of innovative symbolist poets, had been purged, losing their lives to execution, suicide or illness.

However, Lia Sturua was never one of those Georgian women poets whose voices were silenced by the Soviet system or else restricted to writing for children. During Soviet times, she was hardly ever published as the bold character of her subject matter was considered too provocative. As well as the content, her adoption of free verse was unacceptable within the framework of the Georgian literary canon. However, she stubbornly continued writing regardless of the heavy criticism she received from those Soviet writers who represented the prevailing Socialist Realism. She was even accused of perverting young people with her so-called 'Sturuaizm' (a word derived from her surname Sturua) reflecting the many controversial aspects of her poetry.

In one of her interviews, she says, 'I continued writing and wrote what I wanted and in the way I wanted to write about it'. Lia Sturua was one of the pioneers and early masters of free verse in Georgian and played an important role in the development of contemporary Georgian poetry. This is particularly apparent in the work of a group of young Georgian women poets who came to prominence after the collapse of the Soviet Union, such as Diana Anphimiadi, Rusudan Kaishauri and Nato Ingorokva. These poets are featured in our co-translated anthology *A House with No Doors: Ten Georgian Women Poets* (Francis Boutle, 2016).

We began work on translating this selection of Lia's poems in 2021. Once again, war, the plight of refugees, and questions of nationalism are writ large. Against this backdrop, the reading and writing of poems both echoes and changes our responses. Of course, the quotidian and the domestic continue alongside global events, and the so-called ordinary, as poets have always known, is full of depth, mystery and glimpses of the divine. Lia's poems rarely allude directly to political situations but hint at them with references to the motherland and its barbaric flag, and a red dress, like the revolution, confined to a wardrobe.

The forward motion in her poems and their universality comes from her use of images of time, space, colours, seasons, temperatures, music, the body, and mythological figures. These images are multifaceted, both universal and personal. She conveys them through numerous literary tropes such as metaphors, personifications, and many others, often simultaneously, giving her poems a multiplicity of associations.

> There have been so many staircases in my life!
> Especially one, a self-satisfied
> marble staircase,
> somewhere, leading to the middle of nowhere,
> to tragedy, Euripides,
> where women don't hold bottles of milk at their breast
> but kill their children.

In Lia's poems, motion and time are ultimately associated with memory. The family photograph albums are memory concretised and everything eventually transforms into memory. Subjectivity is acknowledged as she writes, 'memory is far too selective'.

One of the few specific memories described in these poems concerns the so-called Dry Bridge. This is considered a shameful reminder of the turbulence of the 1990s in the new countries of the Former Soviet Union. Dry Bridge was a place where impoverished citizens came to sell anything they could in order to survive. In her poem, Lia Sturua equates the selling of ancestral heirlooms with the selling of the motherland, noting however 'if you come here to sell your motherland,/ it is not considered treason'.

Lia Sturua has a particularly deep concern for poets and the difficult process of writing poems. Her metaphors here are complex, empathetic, and often unexpected. She compares the bitterness of creation with stinging water, boiling water, and neuroses. Words for Lia can be numbers, cold and hot, they can be colours which create shades and shadows, and also harmony. The poet is like a conductor but 'it's difficult to conduct, if one of the violins doesn't love you.'

Lia is concerned with the idea of the unbearable fate of poets and yet, her poems are often humorous, a trait which conveys a confusingly tragic sensation in a poem:

> What if you dipped an impoverished poet in plaster
> and stood him there?
> He's always wanted to be a monument.
> He can't find a rhyme for his kidney,
> let alone anyone to buy it.
> Only another impoverished poet
> would be up for buying such inconsistency.

The title of this book, and Lia's 2014 collection, *On the Contrary* speaks to the power of poetry to hold what Carl Jung termed 'the tension of opposites.' The poems take us in one direction and simultaneously in another. Lia often uses architectural imagery, and we can enter her poems like houses, through the front door, or the back door, seeing new views from different windows.

The self, too, is many-chambered and in these poems, the body becomes a flexible assembly of parts. The poet carries a heart in her pocket, her spine is conflated with a block of flats, blood and red wine are outpoured. And this poet-self is generative. In the poems, she is constantly creating, whether children, paintings, or, reflexively, poems, as well as evoking and responding. In this world, each form exists in a version of the others. The interior of the poet-self is invoked by chairs, tables and staircases, but these are not mere objects. They are ensouled and act with agency in the world.

Lia's sensibility is synesthetic, poems are personified, as is music, painting, and weather. She sees the colours of music and poetry. In the final poem of this selection, the whole world comes alive.

Lia Sturua's poems with their allusions and metaphors, alongside the notoriously difficult forms of the Georgian verb, which she employs in a masterful fashion, constitute an ultimate challenge for translators. However, in spite of the choices and compromises necessary for translation, we hope every reader will find something that speaks to their humanity in these remarkable poems.

Natalia Bukia-Peters & Victoria Field

Poems

from *On the Contrary* (2014)

Second Hand Shop

It's as if I carry my heart in my pocket,
while the main pump remains in the body,
the one that followed the soul,
that's the one I am talking about,
with its blood,
the one responsible for emotions.
The pocket is more mysterious
than a collar, or pleats,
children sat in my pockets too,
until I was sure I had milk.
Whom should I breastfeed with blood then?
Those children who were aborted?
But their mouths are bigger than their bodies,
like those on a drawing by a madman
and the screaming decibels
in God's ears
aren't heard, but seen:
when the thrill spirals out
of a cut lemon,
from the bloody pockets – children
with infirmities of scissors,
with the taste of iron in the mouth,
which I will replace with bread,
bread being tender for the oesophagus,
for the rest for the body too: circles,
sticks, pockets for hearts -
the shop selling second-hand children.

I am falling apart. The broken pieces
are scattered around the chair.
What if I bend down, reassemble
them into the familiar layout?
My spine doesn't permit me,
it's happened before, but imperceptibly:
adrenaline did its job, cells
multiplying,
anomalous, like poisonous trees;
you must be pregnant with something:
either a child, or a seedling
you can't fit under a microscope.
A spotlight tears you from the chair,
surrounded by fragments of broken body,
neuroses hang in the air like winter flies,
your final thought is so silly,
you think the chair has a soul.

***

Do you know what might happen at night?
They may raise the bridge,
trap a bird inside it,
the arc of its flight
inscribed there as a memorial.
Their same hands
may grab a peach saved for the morning
and the light may leach from the room.

When you're sad,
the pain stabbing you in the stomach
passes over the bones without touching them.
What is you want, lukewarm favours
with pink librettos in the middle?
Or would you rather have strictness
so you walk like well-trained parallel lines.

***

It is such a winter
where it makes sense to pour boiling water
into an orange-coloured cup,
it's windy every day,
it settles down leaving teeth marks on the trees,
their bark hurts.
When you walked with them,
the wind was billowing,
you sit at home and think flatly,
like a stone, you chant multiplication tables.
If there were a man somewhere,
sharing your solitude,
he wouldn't make you
lean your belly against the mountain.
Children create plural numbers,
they grow and leave,
they also take away with them that time
when the trees were rustling in the moon.

On Plato's Motives

There were such frozen wastes lying in my flesh,
it would have been better to excise them,
those empty places on the map are necessary,
they'll call them 'Terra Incognita'
and they'll discover them,
present you as a New World.
Look, what kind of state will you create
from a multitude of refinements and styles?
And if you let the poets in?
They will arrange such literary pop-art,
on an empty stomach,
it won't be possible to distinguish,
what's smoked fish wrapped in newspaper,
or syntax surprised by Mount Elbrus.
Your lawful house,
where you measure the height of the wall
by a child's crying,
the red dress unworn for ages –
the well-pressed revolution in the wardrobe...
But what kind of frozen wastes were lying on your flesh?
Or what do poets have to do with an ideal world?

Who Are You Now?

To Elguja

Red wine's warming cold crystal,
come on, let's dine
on Flemish Old Masters!
I spread my tired flesh
on the chair.
You'll hang your soul in the air
and I'll ask you, who are you now?
Are you the wind carrying a birds' bouquet
to God?
Are you the heavy burden of grief
that broke your back,
but in reality, had no weight?
Who did you meet there?
Poets sweet as eggnog,
or crude thieves,
can the air lose its teeth?
Can you imagine
how my arm stiffened
when I filled it with your pulse?
No fruit with a worm,
nor one with a square-shaped core,
can change it, nor make me jump
on the broken line of a heart attack!
I'm inclined to simplicity:
the revolution no longer excites me,
when painting, I scatter crumbs
for the birds and feed you,
satiated, you'll rise to such heights,
that, perhaps, you'll discover
the nervous system of the azure sky
and you may recollect that in my head
broken wires need to be replaced...
One more thought tears through me,
perhaps, I will pour my own blood
from my body,
no longer gushing, rhesus negative,

but still living,
like they pour wine,
red wine into a cold glass,
their hearts growing warm in anticipation.

Human Voice

I call directory enquiries,
in order to hear the voice of a human being,
I don't imitate anyone, not even Cocteau!
Everyone has their own version of silence
with more or less bitterness.
First, verbosity, eloquence,
lectures on the barricades of the lecterns,
above, quotations from poems
like drops of blood,
his claim to be single, rings on his fingers,
all of these concern existence.
I cling to the weeds.
She calls the man who abandoned her,
but he's somewhere drinking coffee,
speaking about lilacs, as if describing a woman
and, on the contrary, plays with aesthetics!
I call directory enquiries,
where they only give out
the numbers of the living.

The Twelfth Floor

Winter is coming,
my skeleton became visible
a multi-storey spine
hatching whole families.
My ribs are hurting...
On the road,
I gather relationships,
as if I am collecting taxes,
I pay with my body:
their knife, my neck,
more adrenaline than blood,
meeting God on an empty stomach,
the gusting of ghosts
of bread and fish ...
they missed the table –
how can they become material again?
I enter the house
and say to the sour-smelling air:
'My nobody, how tired I've become.'

Without Shadows

The sun knows
it has all the time in the world, that's why
it burns lazily, days merging
in an unchanged environment
don't have a bitter bite,
aging, too, not destructive,
scratches you softly, whispering,
liver spots, stiff backs...
but after that, death.
Traditional families don't explode,
remnants of colours on a battered palette,
they don't cry out, when, in wholeness,
they simply shone like the sun
confident they'd last forever ...
If I shelter from the coming rain,
they'll punish me with memory.
So, I get stuck directly
in the middle of a trial,
no anaesthesia, no shade nor favours.
It's such an uncivilised space,
but the motherland,
her screaming colours -
her barbaric flag.

***

We survived the winter!
everyone says joyfully,
but summer's no less difficult
to get through.
The trees have their shadows severed,
days, like an anthem,
are tall, full of pathos.
The sun with its hands on its heart
is my mother,
but she couldn't have borne me without trees,
she couldn't have forced me
to stand with my clothes inside out
in the bald heat of the city,
to believe the moon is my father
with such a weak character ...
The tree's more compassionate than both,
above all, it will drop its leaves on me,
soften the soil for me...

Chamber Music

I step over Clementi's sonatas
like an alphabet,
the moon illuminating me,
I wasn't allowed to approach Bach,
the X-ray showed
the spine's weakness
at the music lesson
inscribed by a golden circle,
My curiosity concerning space
ended up as a chamber,
skilful fingers jumped
like mother of pearl buttons
in a polonaise, beaming light,
you had to sacrifice your whole body
to Bach, including the spine,
you had to bear the pain in your head
and be patient.
But who would allow you to approach Bach,
the pianist, him with the stone chin,
or your grandmother, ascending the slope,
a limping luminary.

Requiem

I've somehow become like those
who eat not only the food but the plates too,
the golden ribbons
popping out of their mouths –
they walk by this light,
while I bump into every corner
and obstacle,
so my face would be erased,
so God would invite me to Himself,
would replace
depleted flesh
with enamel plates,
put me back together from the beginning,
and point out to the dwellers of paradise:
Here is a woman who
was consumed by sorrow!
An army of people with gold teeth
attended my funeral,
and listened to Mozart,
exhumed from a mass grave.

***

Sometimes, you get used to people,
as you do to objects, or bread,
their everydayness,
sometimes, you make a discovery and run away,
realising you don't want things to become ordinary.
When I met you,
I was consumed by guilt,
another word for strangeness,
as for you, you saw books in my head,
you opened one
and found a poet who'd been murdered
and afterwards, you expressed your condolences
over and over again,
you illuminated me with the sun at such an angle,
my hair shone enchantingly,
but the encephalogram doesn't lie.
That's what you wanted, to have the truth confirmed,
so you could get away quickly,
but you couldn't leave, you couldn't escape.

There

How many miles of wine did my father walk
to reach my mother as sober as the dawn?
How sharp you are,
quotation in marble from Michelangelo!
And me, once thorns...
Is anyone interested in what it is,
this art of insomnia, the writing of a poem?
There, that cloud
has a long neck
like the cathedral in Alaverdi.
God! Join us in holy matrimony,
what we failed to do here on earth...

2

Where is there an accurate drawing
of the arches and vaults in the brain,
or even of this street?
How many trees, how many houses,
how many bricks, were taken out of the head
to strengthen these walls!
What sadness follows
the intense antidote of sunshine!
How long will you walk with this prosthesis of sadness,
scoring points
as autumn slumps into winter?
The sisters and brothers of mercy
would stand by you on both sides,
under one condition:
you must give the moon
from the silver store
to the brothers and sisters
who have wolves
in the mouths of their ambulances.
What about the genetics of sadness?
Which generation am I,
with how many additives in the blood?
Where is there a precise
and honest plan,
at least of this street?
God, remove just one archway from my brain,
creating something like space, the possibility of air,
otherwise the windows
press against my forehead,
and it hurts.

Poetic Licence

I only read musical notations,
I no longer listen to music,
but even on paper, it flies,
all five lines end with a bird
and ascend to the sky on Saturday.
When it finished
the creation of the world,
it had no more material on hand
and was so consumed by sadness,
that again it had to freeze on the sky
like a porcelain saucer.
Perhaps that's when
God created music?
How this metaphysics helps me
not to bang my head against the wall,
to be able to speak, as I once did
in a measured way
with a controlled, even voice,
which will never be broken,
and will never reveal a naked falsetto.

***

What have I done?
I cut my veins
and instead of blood,
moss poured out.
Is it possible to slit veins
to cook a soup made of moss
for my skinny child?
Mother, you know better
the laws of self-sacrifice.
Ever since my father broke his leg
and I fell from his shoulders,
he's been sitting in a wine glass,
singing about that slippery road,
where he abandoned me like a flower.
Now, for him I've become a stone,
which can crush the flower,
my mother's brain is famished
and it's only with pills
I can express my concern for her.
I'm much more the child of my grandmother,
my eyes trained to beauty,
and because of that,
they kill again.

Vanity

After supper, they brought
ice and silver spoons
to the table
which they put around my sweet memory,
then they drank
and left the table,
that's how he loved me in a lukewarm way.
When they touched each other
with their hot flesh
or cold minds,
I sat at the table
treading water.
They remember that better
than wrinkles, laughter lines
or the awkwardness of an ear
on the oval of a face,
details which turned me
into an epitaph of pain,
they played around a bit with poetry ...
if a conversation begins
about the forgotten culture,
they will bring me back together again
with ice,
so that my memory
won't go rancid like butter.
Nothing else has changed in me,
when they touch one another with body or brain,
or even with anger,
I sit alone at the table,
treading water.

***

Did you fashion these shoes
from the orthopaedic climate?
You put steps inside,
they're so soft,
I won't be able to climb the stairs in my shoes.
The model of a mountain stands nearby
with a sky of crepe de chine,
heartbreakingly inaccessible,
but with traditional wooden panelling,
or should we say, the ceiling?
You hit your head against it in order to make a hole
and from your brain,
a fire escape emerges.
I assume this metaphor springs from a neurosis
but it creates such a space for itself.
If you remove the vowels,
they'll reach the sky,
you'll construct a screaming
skyscraper in the street.
It is clear from here
that there are no ceilings nor panelling,
just the ebb and flow of eternity
from a half-unused brain.

***

Every day
Is just like the last one,
especially with such leafiness
whose quantity doesn't calm you down
but almost incites you
to build a hill of snow at your feet.
The colour white doesn't suit me at all,
it washes my character from my face,
you could paint a landscape or a portrait on it,
either would do,
it would completely capture me
if we didn't share the same blood group,
these trees and me,
the branches in my wounds wouldn't be visible,
nor the children in the trees,
the trees and I united by the shimmering light,
and the other things we have in common.

from *Wolf Hour* (2016)

Until When?

There are two of you in the house:
you and the writing table.
If there's light in between,
everything will work out for you.
Hedonism belongs to a different table,
the round polished one,
it's here too, but
it's moved out of your circle of vision,
perhaps because you're on a diet?
If you don't shed some flesh,
you won't be able to live in the light,
not even for that single moment
when everything comes together.
Is that why domesticity is like climbing a mountain?
Then, falling with such speed,
the floor's in your face
or that very table is!
How will you grow your flesh then? Metaphorically?
Whatever's not included in the diet
because of literary calories
brings us back again to ... Hedonism?
The road of associations, pure silk,
with dead ends in the lining,
which is the saddest?
There you are again, the writing table
with light in between,
for how much longer can you do it?

Staircases

There have been so many staircases in my life!
Especially one, a self-satisfied
marble staircase,
somewhere leading to the middle of nowhere,
to tragedy, Euripides,
where women don't hold bottles of milk at their breast
but kill their children.
Would my mother have done that?
If the circumstances were right?
For example, in such a tragedy: she and I,
two disturbed sopranos,
unfaithful father behind the scenes,
the only property, a red vineyard.
Did he abandon her in the dressing room?
Hack her into pieces
while sweetening the next one?
Did he sell this poor red one
to Van Gogh?
His treachery and my acapella!
But what will be my fate
when perfect pitch overflows from my ears?
For example, I can't even sing in the chorus.
My mother could at least have broken the bottle
in her breasts, so I'd eat glass,
so I wouldn't be so sharp
and categorical but I know
that even if I bring her ten chariots of the sun,
she won't fly,
even after death she's still afraid,
on the staircase of thoughts which lead nowhere
where joints are also joining in ...

They See It Like That[3]

The madman comes and as if from a book
of anatomical curiosities
paints me an ear the size of a town,
he imitates no one, never repeats anything,
he's not normal after all.
From where does he demand
undiluted music among the listeners?
When my homework's
a crack in the ceiling, a creaking door:
following the text with my finger
and after that, hungry at first,
then, changing intonation,
then, shrieking to the sky,
accompanied by cracks,
I work in the direction of pain...
I read a novel with refrains
and think how you really wanted a poem
but instead, ended up writing a thousand pages!
You watch the same amount of music,
from the comfort of a private box
an unsullied concert
performed by the listeners.
The reader's eyes have perfect pitch:
they know how to leave a line of light in the door,
see the starched spectator in the baroque box
and when this public velvet is ripped from them,
conscience is also possible
through the eyes of madmen and poets
who see things this way...

Rain, Almost Musical

Rain, almost musical,
wearing a black tailcoat, doesn't follow fashion,
the orchestra changed too,
it no longer has its hand on its forehead,
as if gasping for the last drop of air
in its throat,
this collective madman is suffocating ...
I'm offering sympathy with words.
Crows are flying, wet and heavy,
like black sacks
so, if I pile them
one on top of the other,
they'll become for me a monument of the day
when I desire death.
Not wanting to play that day's game,
when you put your cheek against a train
and the wind starts blowing,
and when the same cheek
forms a corner with the pillow of such bliss
you end up sighing,
and instead, you face the orchestra and breathe!
Where the crows are - empty eye sockets!
They will look at me
and I'll wear a smile
from the year before last...

Again, On The Theme Of Plants

You left.
In my dream, half of the bed of me was broken,
but in a better dream I become whole,
one side of me is snowy earth,
on the other side, a plant is growing out of me,
warmed up by the ordinary process of inflammation,
a sign? A warning?
Why so much sky?
There's little soil but is it used efficiently
when preparation's done in the head?
The ear, a shell easily crushed,
is lying on such difficult music,
I need time, so that there'll be a word,
after the melting snow of versification...
Why, when there is lightning?
When there are Heineken umbrellas in the street,
bodies blossoming like grasslands,
such orange details you would have added!
From the shimmering of mandarins,
from the girls seen with the serious children...
Oil paint is risky,
you wouldn't lay next to a woman like a water colour,
she'd spoil your style,
you know, even with this stupefied flesh,
I can still bear a winter blended with spring,
stinging, a nettle in the brain!
In other words, it's the plant theme again,
I continue to tell my blossoming lies,
I don't know to what extent ...

Late Autumn[4]

Do you wish you weren't a prisoner of your mood?
Take some metres of yellow,
the same amount of blue and create a field
in your boring house.
When music takes flight
and you can no longer produce it,
children, real and yet to be born,
distribute your stressful poems
to depict this conflict.
How many tubes of paint must you squeeze,
in order to get a vulgar red?
To have enough for screaming, the first step,
then a paragraph, then you begin yourself,
scream, full stop, scream, full stop,
you'll leave the house during one of the pauses.
The wall you ate in your childhood,
will wave its hand at you, you lacked lime,
or the white colour, you still don't know today...
perhaps you lacked the wind too,
and the feeling after flying?
Like a familiar and forgotten poem,
on the muddy bread, potato, the air of a paragraph,
then you begin yourself, the earth so yellow you panic,
reducing poems to jelly,
zeros of snow ... a lie no longer exists,
or, in other words, were there no breaks
for those crazy ancestors
who were against the norms of that time?

Dramatic Personae

I have never had
many characters in my life.
They just hung around casually.
They came and left.
On the old red trams, they kept handkerchiefs[5]
in their pockets, those closer to the heart.
Women, near the church,
emerged from their tired shoes,
awakened from a white night,[6]
like a dawn breaking,
a crowd of them speaking
their hedgerow dialect,
these women struggle to conduct
their musical parts in the chorus.
Who is in the leading role?
Why am I asking?
Was it me who eliminated the hero?
And now I want someone to pour
milk into the night,
for the day be long,
so I'm not afraid of my bed,
not to speak to me in simplified text,
from behind the wall,
not to let them see how I lean
against the poetry citations
and cry... I want all of these,
but I couldn't invent them.
My memory prompted me,
blood, redder and quicker,
my cardiogram started jumping,
I made my swollen liver two fingers smaller,
the printing house stopped printing my book,
I couldn't create a hero, nor a role.
For minor roles, chairs will do.
A bed, a writing table,
are perfectly good characters.
Or those, on the lost trams, with red handkerchiefs
in their pocket? It's true though,

that death has flattened them.
Nevertheless, they still come,
printing the paper as dawn breaks.
I also understand the language of the dead
when a branch grows from their mouth.

Dry Bridge or 'Buy Something!'[7]

Dry Bridge doesn't straddle the water,
it has no geography.
If you come here to sell your motherland,
it's not considered treason.
It's cheaper than a two-bedroomed apartment,
but painful as both legs being amputated.
Two obelisks are for sale!
What if you dipped an impoverished poet in plaster
and stood him there?
He's always wanted to be a monument.
He can't find a rhyme for his kidney,
let alone anyone to buy it.
Only another impoverished poet
would be up for buying such inconsistency.
Is that desire for fame paradoxical
or the social motivation
in a hungry poet's creative oeuvre?
Children trained in this topic
are born as easily as pebbles
planted deep in the walls of universities,
chest-high to the Bachelor students,
up to the necks of the Masters.
If you dipped them in golden water,
they'd appraise themselves as antiquities.
An investor will come and drop the river
between their thighs.
Eighty percent of locals are suicidal,
they're afraid of the earth, water's a softer killer.
Come and buy the river,
it's already been bottled!
My phone's switched on,
I'm on the line!

The Lie of the 'Constructor'[8]

First, normal parents built a house,
then children,
if they strain their imagination,
they may manage to create a garden too.
The cosmic gossiping of sun and moon,
about participating in all this business
shines a light, but doesn't shed warmth...
normal children keep coming back
to a problem that's been chewed over and over:
They build a family from the Constructor,
and people like me build volcanoes!
The principle is the same, the lies are more,
if it weighs too much, it will lead me to a man,
whose gestures accelerate,
wide strokes of an artist's brush, tense colours.
It's hot next to him!
Why has he left? So that the rinsed fog
wouldn't solidify in his eyes, or so he wouldn't see,
how I went back to building volcanoes?
The bile erupting from them,
at the time my liver turns to autumn?
I pacify parents who are stuck
somewhere in a dream: an awkward red lava
isn't included the Constructor's instructions,
nor does anyone tell me any more:
it's hot next to you!

Wolf

What came out of it?
They brought a postmodern moon
into the sky, allocated a castrated dog
for self-assertion
and they got an operatic howling.
The bells of fear
aren't written in the musical score of the city.
Postmodernism's a theft that's permitted!
If you fall asleep at the writing table,
they'll remove the half-baked words,
an ear for assonance and many more things,
apart from that wolf which you have in your body,
ripping you apart and refusing refinement.
But why a wolf, in any case?
It's cold in silk underwear,
stereotypical velvet causes allergy,
the moon in the tea cup
is an imitation of that real one,
hanging in the provinces,
which has its own wolves,
one of them myself.
When your sweetheart lies in the earth,
there's only howling!
Not an ounce of sentimentality,
half a step away from forgery!
It will catch up somewhere and bothers him,
He also has an ear for assonance,
a quick eye, where my wolf
wears himself out, rubs, breaks down.
If only it didn't resemble a neutered dog,
with a domesticated high voice singing,
let's say, up to the ceiling,
When in the amplitudes of howling, there are so many orchestras,
and such attentive light from the moon!
They can't help it
but they understand each other...

Am I late?

Your eyes have been switched off, I'm told,
there's no one to be seen inside them,
if no one looks out, except for cars,
my head has agoraphobia,
you have to screw arms and legs onto the body
every time you go out.
I'm also afraid of the house,
wondering, which corners belong to the spiders
and which to the punished children?
Night insects rustle the air,
they finish their geography
with the sources of light,
I finish it with an aggressive street,
which leads to you.
The lopped limbs of the trees
look like cheeks in motion.
If they don't chew people like me,
they won't be able to produce oxygen
for children and their children's children...
Fear's contagious. I will consume its bacteria,
the elevated pose of decadence, the attempt at normality,
I will take it three times a day,
I will swallow it with water and will come to you.

City Squares

An energy-saving lamp is lit in my head,
where cold children are curled up,
I neither warm them up nor calm them down,
I throw them straight into a poem,
as if into the baptismal font,
myrrh has an effect on some of them
and they turn into poets,
most of them become discontented,
they organise demonstrations,
you can't stop them with the flying logic,
the kind of logic applied only by children
before they become people,
in other words, metaphors, this is my army,
they have eaten my brain,
the earth of the planet, where the southern cities
are marked with blood,
the northern ones, with red banners,
which command me
to surrender myself to children who'll eat me
and make me appoint them as luminaries!
The anatomy textbook rots in my stomach,
people run around carrying the city squares,
those squares that were positively round
before the revolution.
The ideal ones.

The Day Off[9]

The day off!
Where is it coming off from, from loneliness?
I hammer in the nails
(I'm making a new head),
more than half the strikes hit my fingers,
Passers-by will hang on my involuntary shrieks.
What's the big deal if there's dissonance in the ear!
The street could do with some surprise,
and me, the attention behind the wall,
its interior option, to be on the verge of tears,
the positive degree of curiosity,
everything apart from compassion,
which was eaten by moths...
If the street had not played its role,
if it had lifted the cars into the trees,
the pavements into the rooves, to arouse inspiration,
I would not have made a new head for myself
according to the old principle, that when the features are regular
they'll make you look better, but for what?
For the false promises of days off?
The working days eat me like moths,
successfully, as sorrow is pure wool,
in the silence of a day off I can hear,
my hair and nails growing, like they do on a corpse...

February

I am good at talking to the dead,
so what should I tell you?
I began using worn-out words more often
in my vocabulary in connection with you:
it's difficult, I find it hard, I can't cope
with my own self, memory, autumn...
It's even more difficult to play
at being self-contained:
yes, a musical score on the page
has the appearance of legitimacy,
I walk under attentive eyes,
a voice crushed by stones
certainly shouldn't be heard,
a child, however far she might go,
still looks out from my hip,
her husband died, her child
grew on my second hip,
I walk like a flowering lilac,
someone should admire me in spring!
Do such things happen in your heaven?
Such things don't happen in my world either,
I invented them,
like a sunny day...

Awkward Geography

The circle of crying is tied up
in your middle
there's not even a dot,
the prick of a compass on the paper,
its flat environment...
In order to return you to three dimensions,
they have to repeat the circle into a sphere,
on a relief map, here and there,
they have to make churches jump out,
if they use more salt on the bulging place,
they'll end up with either a mountain
or a poet, there's no sphere
without the occasional scarlet inhabitants,
you're born from their screams,
when you cannot see the sky anymore,
if the crow doesn't fly over it and underline it,
sacrifice your dots!
Elongate the outline,
and a man will peep out from the ellipsis of a peach,
he'll demand the name of the revolutionary,
but anyway, your south is faraway,
here the circumference is cut with a knife,
when the blood is seen on you from one side of the sun...

from the *Literary Gazette*

(December 2016)

***

She appeared naked, smooth, marvellous
and the creased dress departed.
The forms are screaming,
even if you drape them with fabric,
the volume sags. Only the wrinkles
remain loud. Only the curtain.
And if the impression of a stage-set is created,
that's the end of truth. More precisely,
closed minds will block the imagination.
And what are the wrinkles hiding?
Authentic origin? Is that dangerous?
But the family albums are here, aren't they?
Where she is still naked, smooth, marvellous,
transformed into memory,
and memory is far too selective...

***

From noon until two in morning,
my day is in black and white.
That pink thing I used to have,
with its cheek like a peach,
has fulfilled its role of being a target.
It's over, everything obvious is over,
as if your finger's stuck in the door,
and the opposite vowels hurt.
You've got the light on at two in the morning,
just you, and someone else opposite.
You are in love with those two windows.
They immediately betray you:
you can't compare your faded pink
to the sexiness of a field of poppies.
When you were a target, someone
would throw a knife at you,
someone else, a stone,
somebody liked you so much
his eyes were nailed to the peach tree.
Loneliness was only a number
not a way of life, from twelve noon
until two in the morning,
who misses you, who remembers you,
who needs you?
You stand and count those windows with lights on,
if one of those devoted friends still loves you,
they will say:
The peach smothered her with a blossom.
That's what they will say, afterwards.

***

Winter, sad snow,
sad enough to be used in a poem,
(but I still don't love you).
In winter other small things help me bear it:
unlawful rain,
the colour orange in its stubbornly major key ...
If you turn a day inside out,
it has such a slippery lining
you'll be unable to wipe your hands clean
and you'll bring both right hands
to your mouth to taste the day's sweetness ...
The face of the day is no longer chic,[10]
in other words, style, sugar on the glossiness,
it's old-fashioned, talentless, timeless,
and if there's no such thing as time,
how would these spaces be filled?
Would you put it in the basement of memory
with the sun, moon and their active silkiness?
It's almost a museum when it's snowing,
one entity, not a poem hooked up to a drip,
orange in its major key also tilts towards the sun,
those lost in time meet each other here,
there are fewer reasons to die in summer.

Saguramo Street

for Duduna and Irina

On my small street,
the Chopins are looking out from the open windows...
Some are not able to see them,
some stop to chat with them.
What about? Probably the sadness of the universe...
What sadness did I have then?
In winter, I missed the light of acacia flowers,
in summer, the subtext of snowballs...
There was always music, they no longer threw those grand pianos
from the open windows
familiar from the stories they told,
but instead, my handsome young uncle
was sent into exile, the freight train
frozen to his right side,
his wife, to his left.
They returned in black and white,
gave birth to children, which, of course
is accompanied by music,
but the kind of music, you get
from throwing a grand piano out of the window
whose owner's emigrated,
as you move to a different house
and every night you hear an elderly militiaman's
spirit speak to the soul of your cat,
or maybe you don't move anywhere at all,
but feel pity for these accomplished lines,
uniting the houses with the sky,
the sky to the churches, that were erased, destroyed...
What does Chopin want
with these nameless, senseless windows?
Why does the Conservatoire exist?
You already know so much about sadness.
The ear-of-the-street would not be sufficient
to ease it but would lighten you up.
But the street no longer exists, it's been consumed
by the temperamental stadium next door.

***

I walk, stretching out the road home,
the road is on its own, I too am alone,
the twenty-four-hour pharmacy is illuminated,
so that the healing parts of plants
emerge from the medicines...
If only my window was lit up the way
it was when I was capable of admiration!
I'd be rapturous, a hymn, a cappella,
a symphony orchestra!
Only chamber music is sufficient for the single light,
the yellow line trapped by the door,
at low volume, there's quiet joy,
somebody's in the house, and if no one's home,
a familiar sadness, a genteel despair,
awaits me with chattering teeth
and, today, that's the reality...

Attempting to Love

When the illusion of a breast made of rock
eats half of life,
whatever remains isn't measured in days,
but by suffering,
by how well it fitted a poetic form.
Did you lie down with this aesthetic,
or with real bones?
The rock is nature, it will take what you offer,
but should you love it so much
you twist your neck?
It won't pity you, nor will it
kick up such a tornado of words
that the wind pushes them into your face.
It will look with your blood,
rock is rock, it thinks straight,
it can't turn the corner safely,
it doesn't have your flexibility, nor a car's ability to manoeuvre.
When you collide with each other,
if you survive, the wall awaits you,
if not, then a picture, the grave at long last...
Why are you in the earth?
Insist on cremation in a neighbouring country
and return to the rock.
Hard, steep, abrupt,
poor epithets, but related,
when you adorn them with blood,
Gothic, aflame!
You'll adjust your eyes but not your liver,
not with the black pepper of the nation,
certainly not with ashes from the stove,
it's not necessary to use pathos
but what does a breast made of rocks rest on?
On the exclamation marks from
my literary past? What blindness!
When you want to be moss underfoot,
small, modest, but fitting ...[11]

Our Daily Bread[12]

The bread I didn't eat,
I did not spice up the amber of the dish,
Once, in a dream, I saw, more precisely, absence of bread:
there was none at home, none in the shops,
it was wartime, war itself was hungry:
it walks on the flesh of the Bible, or Gospels,
bread should know, where to put its foot down on Matthew,
where on John, and also
that a nail is loyal to the plank,
God is responsible for bread.
If you eat an apple from a fresco,
partially responsible for the word,
only not the printed one,
where, then, do the black printed flowers come from?
Treason, pain, nailed places,
are on me, when I read,
I might have missed the correction,
a small falsehood,
the main thing is they believe the text!
The war is over, bread will be heaped high on the counters.
Gluttony from God!
Also from Him, a mountain which will immediately erupt,
and, if it is pointed, cry out,
its sad recitative suits the longevity of the field.
Why? Question marks are like shadows
in the summer sun, but the sun is stronger,
at least, I think, from here....

from *Arali* magazine (2016)

It Warms Me So Deeply

I don't know how trees love each other,
nor do I know how they surrender to spring,
nor do I know anything about pain either.
They give birth to greens without hesitation,
which I can only do
by mixing yellow and blue.
It's so like me to complicate something,
to hesitate, to look suspiciously,
even though I'm stronger than my own body.
I can't drown the sadness caused by this thought
in wine with Georgian clay in its depths
that will not mix with unreality,
but what if I yield to tea,
to the orange Chinese dynasty?
Three line silence will grow in height,
the mountains will create a mood to match mine,
especially if I'm standing on a precipice
and the end of the world is at my feet,
when my mother's blue-rimmed glass
is so real you can see it, feel it warming your hand.
Trees surrender to the wind, to spring, without hesitation,
the birds sing with an urban accent,
the earth inclines to the dialect,
I thought I knew better,
always lay on my side, from birth,
If I loved someone, in the middle,
when I had children, words sprouted like poppies
in order to prove that I was not less motherly?
It warms me so deeply, I know even
in comparison with the blue rimmed clay,
but the glass is screaming.
But what can I do about that,
that the glass is warm and screams?

***

First, the man leaves, then
his address dies to you,
along with its sweet doctrines,
keep it in memory,
avoid the cliché of taking flight.
When you use numbers as words,
there are two voices: cold and warm,
like colours. Shades
create one another
from the hither and thither of harmony.
The water in the fridge looks at me
with stinging nettles,
the boiling water, with neuroses,
the murdered children appease with velvet -
how spiteful!
No blood is shed in a battle of looks,
but when an orchestra's playing in your poem,
it's difficult to conduct it,
if one of the violins doesn't love you...

Notes

1 **I am falling apart...** (p. 10)
In the last two lines, Lia plays with the letter 's'. In Georgian, 'sisulele' means 'silliness', 'suliereba' means 'spirituality' and 'suli', 'soul'.

2 **Where is there...** (p. 24)
The poem contrasts the purity and beauty of silver with the wildness of wolves, especially the idea of them howling to the moon.

3 **They See It Like That** (p. 35)
The poem refers to 'the entertaining anatomy' which we understand to be a series of books describing anatomical curiosities.

4 **Late Autumn** (p. 38)
In this poem, flying is a metaphor for poetry.

5 **Dramatic Personae** (p. 39)
The Georgian reads 'red tram handkerchief'. Lia tells us this is a complex metaphor referencing sadness, specifically around the red trams that no longer run.

6 **Dramatic Personae** (p. 39)
In Georgian, a white night is an idiomatic way of describing insomnia.

7 **Dry Bridge or 'Buy Something!'** (p. 41)
In the 1990s, Dry Bridge in Tbilisi was where the impoverished population sold their possessions, both everyday items and precious ones, such as antiques, fine china, icons, paintings, gold and silver. Foreigners, mainly from the West, bought many of these, and took them abroad.

8 **The Lie of the 'Constructor'** (p. 42)
The Constructor is a Soviet-era children's toy, akin to Lego. The word 'nagveli' has two meanings: bile and sadness.

9 **The Day Off** (p. 46)
The word 'gamosasvleli' means a day off and 'one which comes out'.

10 **Winter, sad snow** (p. 53)
In the phrase 'the face of the day' the Georgian word has several meanings, namely, the right, smooth side of fabric, in front, directly opposite, towards, or on the right.

11 **Attempting to Love** (p. 56)
Cremation is not permitted in Georgia.
In Georgian, the word 'moss' is used where English uses 'straw' in such phrases as 'clutching at straws' or a 'straw for a drowning man' and this is hinted at in the last line.

12 **Our Daily Bread** (p. 57)
A nail is loyal to the plank. Here, Lia is referring to a coffin.

From the Translators

*** indicates 'untitled'. In the Contents we have used title case for those poems Lia Sturua has given titles, and the opening words of those that are untitled.

Wherever possible, we preserved the line-breaks as Lia has them, but have introduced or removed punctuation for clarity. Georgian poets make free use of ellipses and exclamation marks. These can seem stronger in English, and at times distracting, so we have often chosen to omit them.

Five of these poems have already appeared in translation in the parallel-text anthology, *A House With No Doors – Ten Georgian Women Poets* (Francis Boutle Publishers, 2016).

Lia Sturua

Lia Sturua was born in 1939 and is a prominent Georgian poet. She graduated from Ivane Javakhishvili Tbilisi State University's Faculty of Philology. In 1974 she defended her PhD thesis on The Artistic function of Colour in Galaktion Tabidze's Poetry. She lectured at the University and was a senior researcher at the Shota Rustaveli Institute for Georgian Literature. Since 1999 she has been a literature consultant at the Galaktion Tabidze Museum. Her first collection, *Trees in the City* was published in 1962, followed by twelve more books. As well as poetry, Lia Sturua has published prose, including the novels, *Happy Silence, Stone Dropped in Milk,* and *What Ate the Vine?* Her poetry has been translated into German, French, English and Finnish.

Bibliography

On the Contrary, Saunje Publishing, 2014

What Ate the Vine, Intelekti Publishing, 2013

Selection, Diogene Publishing House, 2013

The Forgetting Day, Publishing House Chveni Mtserloba, 2012

The Sea is closed, Siesta Publishing House, 2009

100 Verses, Intelekti Publishing, 2008

Stone Dropped in Milk, Merani Publishing, 2002

One Hundred Sonnets and Others, Merani Publishing, 1999

Happy Silence, Merani Publishing, 1996

Contemplations at the Edge of the Sun, Merani Publishing, 1989

Sonnets, Merani Publishing, 1987

Verses and Poems, Sov. Georgia, 1986

Trees in the City, Nakaduli Publishing, 1962

Literary Prizes and Awards

Honorary award SABA 2017 for the Contribution to the Georgian Literature

Literary award SABA 2013 in category the best poetry collection for *The Forgetting Day*

Shota Rustaveli State Prize 2000 for *One Hundred Sonnets and Others*

Georgian State Award 1995 for her Artistic Work

Galaktion Tabidze Award 1988

This biography is adapted from the website of the Georgian National Book Centre.

About the Translators

Natalia Bukia-Peters is a freelance translator, interpreter and teacher of Georgian and Russian. She studied at Tbilisi State, Ilia Chavchavadze University and holds a Masters degree from Leiden University, the Netherlands. She has been a translator for the Poetry Translation Centre and a member of the Chartered Institute of Linguists in London for several years. Her most recent book is Diana Anphimiadi's *Why I No Longer Write Poems* in collaboration with Jean Sprackland (Bloodaxe, 2022).

Victoria Field is a writer and poetry therapist. Her most recent poetry collection is *A Speech of Birds* (Francis Boutle, 2020). *The Lost Boys* (Waterloo, 2013) won the Holyer an Gof prize for poetry and drama. Her memoir *Baggage: A Book of Leavings* was published by Francis Boutle in 2016. She has co-edited three books on therapeutic writing.

Published joint translations by Natalia and Victoria include *Dictatorship of Poetry* by Zurab Rtveliashvili, *A House with no Doors – Ten Georgian Women Poets* (both Francis Boutle), a book-length collection of short stories, *Me, Margarita* by Ana Kordzaia-Samadashvili (Dalkey Archive), short stories in Dalkey Archive's *Best European Fiction* anthologies, and collections by Dato Magradze from fal publications.